Lover

Poetry

By

Teresa La Dart

AuthorHouse™
1663 Liberty Drive
Bloomington, IN 47403
www.authorhouse.com
Phone: 1-800-839-8640

First published by AuthorHouse   1/12/2010

ISBN: 978-1-4490-4631-6 (sc)

Library of Congress Control Number: 2009911621

Printed in the United States of America
Bloomington, Indiana

This book is printed on acid-free paper.

authorHOUSE®

Thank you for being interested in the context of this book which is dedicated to father, mother, and my companion, Lover. Love is an undeniable entity, and without its inspiration, I fear this book would have been impossible to write. An intense solitude occurred after tragically losing father, my hero, at 18 years old, which coerced me to ponder life at a different angle. But I soon learned more important, it's not the angles you choose in life, but rather the angels. My mother, Virginia, is an angel, but let me warn you, she is a hard headed one, and we are just alike. But seriously, thank you for picking this book up. Poetry may be considered a lost art, but it is still about personal feelings, and I believe that is what makes us human. As you immerse yourself into these words and for a moment live through my poetry, hopefully, you will realize that self love equates to true love, and that is what God is all about.

I now dedicate this book as well to you, my readers, and may all your life be filled with love and tenderness.

Teresa La Dart & Pierre

'Poetry on my mind' 1974

Teresa La Dart is a resident of Southaven, Mississippi.

She currently resides with her new 'Lover', all be him Malti-Poo, 'Pierre'.

With God's guidance, she endeavors to make an extension of herself through poetry.

Believable Magic

When I am with you my love is boundless,
and readily juices flow as sap from a tree!
The outer shroud of my skin sheds its thickness.
I become a slave to your touch and let my soul run free.

Two bodies disappear and are made as one.
Seconds graduate to hours.
You are my warmth and breath - -
This love glows like the sun.
Baby, I'll reply to your every need from tall ivory towers.

For each heartbeat I listen and feel so sad
to think that each beat is one less more.
Each word from your sweet lips is etched in memory.
I want to forever hold you in my arms for this magic I adore!

Beyond The Outer Limits

Each time that our bodies pass by,
flowers follow our paths –
the kind that never die.
Flags seem to fly higher
with news of romance to dress the sky.

How the artistry of this love spans the Outer Limits!
There isn't enough ground here to bond these emotional fulfillments.

Be my equal
and allow excellence to be our goal.
A handle on these aspects shall permit our relationship to grow
over and beyond the Outer Limits
along with Cupid and his bow!

Say "Yes"

My direction in life is not to own you.
The wonderfulness of this love is simply holding on to
saying "Yes" to a generous embrace,
and expressions revealed beneath sensuous eyes of praise.

It seems happiness, on which my very existence depends,
and losing you would be like death dropping in.

But, if I take steps to own you - -
it could force this love to lack strength.
Dare I need you so much as to risk slashing this love's length?

Ask me into your heart.
Mine is on fire.
Making love to you now is all that I desire.

A Search For Peace

Completely lounging away my time
while trying to make a perfect rhyme - -
Cleaning words from this slate anew - -
still to swing only a few.

Lend me a hand, and we'll soon release
a poem to the world in search of peace - -
Wherefore peace would surely announce
love filling our cups, not sparing an ounce.

Then morning would dawn showing an immaculate sun
excited to tell the world "We're one! We're one!"

The Heart Of The Matter

Speaking from the heart - -
this giving we can do.
Fact is, there bears a skill in said giving not to fall apart - -
refined methods of employing our hearts
is to suppress emotions undue.

How to know when we are on the terrace of that moment?
Oh, but our pilots are invisible
and whimsical landings unadvisable.

Voicing from the heart - -
a fragile, learned situation.
More than not recommended though,
for in one's heart matters soul liberation.

Wasted Anticipation

The fragrance of this jar smells of caviar.
I open, hoping to find plenty,
but the contents are empty,
so I toss it into the great garbage afar.

Death's Question

To hug the contents of love
To squeeze the secret of power
To encounter fearfulness of isolation
To liege to society and its promises
To flee from the murky nightfall
To beg pardon of high authority
To philosophize with abstractness of life - -

The queasy stages of growing old - -
Will they really end at death?

Why?

Why I fell in love?
Maybe I'll never know.
I clung to wild contrition's
that his feelings would finally show.

It was a kind of home where a woman's psyche took rest,
and not without a garden where I danced with him undressed.

What stopped the music?
Its energy grew hollow in my ears.
Like some animal who is put to sleep,
a sudden darkness now appears.

So I'll make that special effort to know why I fell in love . . .
hoping I won't be bored with emptiness that life is not made of.

Your Love

What sincerity in thou face!
How illuminated with grace!
What devotion in your caress!
Never, Never to suppress!

Whatever could persuade me to feel
that your love is unreal?

Character - Your #1 Mate

Making improvements on your character - -
hence, variations in one's personality will bring
a following of friends
and good days with no ends.

Yes, updates on character - -
to ring out the old and ring in the new!
Hell if it will grant you everything, but one thing is for sure ...
there will be less manure at your front door!

Goodness In All

A failure weeps inside
and smiles lightly on the outside.
Fighting repeatedly for acceptance,
his conscience cannot battle reluctance.

Times were once when he was sure,
and this aim he set forth to cure.
Alas, one deed he mistook
set him in the light of his "fellow" man a miserable crook.

Eras may mend his broken will,
But mentally this moment will never stand still.
Give him love.
Give him hope.
God only knows how well he needs both.

A Blended Dare

This life - - an ecstasy of events
of loves who can't even pay the rents.
Prices going up everyday
and surprisingly my interest follows its way.

Feelings like these should be a crime.
I'm caught in the middle - - a slave of my prime.

It's just that night after night
no true love is even close in sight.
Only an affair - -
doing another dare.

The Man Upstairs

Pollution is choking us and God to death.
Have we yet strangled our souls on lust?
Taking our steps before our breath - -
    no breath to waste on what is just.

Meanwhile God's smogged eyes burn red
    as he waits to put us all to bed.

Honest To Goodness

Honest to goodness we all have a heart.
Honest to goodness we all play a part.
Honest to goodness we all have a brain.
Honest to goodness every brain has a strain.

Then how and why do we differ?
Could it be that some use neither?
Might some use one without the other?

Can this misfit be the reason
for all the treason
plotted against our own brother?

Back To Trusting

I wanted to trust this beautiful man
having been impressed by his life style,
so open and grand!

Better than often I conveyed my love
only to be used like a worn out glove.

Today a message was left from that same beautiful man,
but it will go unanswered because I'm trusting again!

My Father
Louis Lucian La Dart, 1946

Louis La Dart, 1961

Louis and Virginia, 1948

Lover

The La Dart family, 1954

From left to right, Joe, Sam, Mother, Father, Teresa, Lucian, Nina

21

After church, 1957

From left to right, Sam, Nina, Joe, Teresa, Lucian

First grandchild, Jennifer, with Grandfather Louis, 1972

"We really made it this far!"
Top left to right, Lucian, Sam, Mother, Joe, Nina, Teresa,
at Sam's 60th birthday celebration.

Our family extension at Sam's 60th birthday celebration

Teresa's one FUN place in time!
DJ days, 1992

Following Along

Trying to find my one place in time
is a chore for me to ever foresee!

God Knows Best

Among the tall wintry trees God and I chatted,
and I asked of God –
"Why does life seem ill combated?"

He said –
"Freedom of the Cosmos lay at your feet."
I replied –
"Yes, but what good is it if only I weep?"

God answered –
"It's your will if predominance of evil forces dresses you with shame."
And standing on the edge of darkness I consumed the blame.

To Be

Exercising faculties of the mind
and intuitive perceptions of the soul
enumerative times of the day you'll find
why adjustment to life is such a demanding role.

Piousness of the soul beseeches
foreign relics within the mind to show
nobility of one's birth which may then be in pieces
miraculously wear an innocent glow.

There are complexities better avoided and some better faced --
most definitely, they cannot be erased.

So live the power of judgment and make it divine
in order that mind and soul can keep body in line.
And never feed it that which may bring harm,
rather that which will keep charismatically warm.

Weeping Willow

To stand beneath this tree of grief - -
To stand and hear this Willow's weep - -
She is noticed to weep for her head is constant
in a sad array of brush adornment.

To attempt to lift her branches a face
would only prove to her the world's disgrace.
Does the Willow weep for causes valid - -
that she should see everything so pallid?

Weeping Willow weeps for all
who make each day without call.
Now Weeping Willow weeps for me
for I have become a part of her tree.

Best Friends

Remember times when back and forth our bodies reeled
with laughter on subjects that from the rest of the world stayed secretly concealed?
Slumber parties spent eating until we could stuff no more,
followed by ghost stories that really happened, we swore.
Do you recall dear daddy's entertainment with the rubber snake? - -
At which point your nerves were all a shake?

When you made that big step to walk down the aisle,
I was in the wedding but forgot to smile.
Helpless I was like a lion in a cage
to save you from a potential mess at such an early age.

Personal confrontations we have had
failed to degrade our friendship, and, by George, I'm glad!
Lots of incidences pettily ensued
have ruined the finest of comrades so tightly glued!
I know when I'm down and feeling amiss,
you're the perfect conversationalist.

A laudatory song I dedicate to you, most trusted friend,
because with us the music never stops, and so together we blend!

One

Today - - what shall it hold for me?
Shall I discover someone new?
And what if I do?
Will that one care
to stop and share?

And would they wonder of ever their trivialities so small
be brought to my call?

And what would tomorrow be like then?
Our love would be ONE!
Strange that yesterday we had none.

Eternal is now our love,
and there shall never be ENOUGH!

Quote Scarlett

If I could be convalesced from tomorrow's fears
storms would cease their pursuits and enthused rainbows would appear.

They would zoom for regions protecting my body
while in proof buying preface to a life un-shoddy.

Back to those fears having shot straight out the window - -
in succession would be achievements legally stealing the show.

Then the cobwebs of fearfulness would altogether fade away
for as measurably small as it seems, 'Tomorrow is another day'!

Hopeless

The perennial task of fixing myself
from jars of makeup atop my shelf - -

Isn't it a pity - -
trying to make myself pretty?

When the end of this task is a shame,
for the beginning and the end always turn out the same.

A Woman On The Move

Covered in a glistening frost of diamonds, the girl became a woman.
A page was turned in the journey from coloring books to a land lest cheap.
The cunning splendor of her youthfulness lacked self discretion.
Yet she was unhappy in this phase,
for it was intimacy she did seek.

A simple calling of her name by some who cared . . .
She was a single female scared silly but always prepared.
God helped her hold onto her morning star through flashes of discontent
from men who plead her company and then left her ego unkempt.

An account was drawn in her mind to improve on selections.
By this age she had convinced herself of life's prized possessions.
So she slips into that lovely white dress because she has finally found
a man who weds her for the woman she is with all else toned down.

The Lighter Side Of Life

Stopping to vie the lighter side of life
hangs a splint of good humor to remedy a day of strife.

What a nice feeling it is to be lively again
while visiting this city of no akin.
Dreamily I paint walls show gay hues in the night - -
portraying impeccable designs, setting atmospheres aright!

There is apt to follow drink and good cheer
as friends gather to party here.
I begin to line streets with gorgeous parades - -
playing out the lighter side of life in momentous charades.

It's time to sigh a farewell to this escape from strife
while in accordance I value fruit yielded from the lighter side of life.

Riddle Of Love

Upon our devotion was born this riddle
of how becoming your love was like silk to a needle.
For after you needled me with an undying passion,
I smoothly went under accepting in fashion!

Second Chance, Please

The care worn wave of this deep darkened tomb
offers no comforting chimes to ease the pit of my womb.

No longer may I engage in eradications with others...
Oh, the pain I have caused to father, mother, sisters, and brothers.

Malediction will now be a stranger to my ears
forever freeing me from many embittered fears.

This foxy compartment which I lie within
contains no jurisdiction to say I've sinned.

A straight seam of life delayed too long to walk
has left me in this deep silent grave with only bugs and worms to talk.

The Lust Of Your Smile

A signal of lust transmitted into full bloom - -
Interesting to say that not a word needed to be spoken.

I was greeting smiles within the room
and strayed at yours which housed an unguarded token.

In the shadow of that token meshed my promiscuous thinking,
and our eyes met in the middle equally distant from unblinking.

My Mother, Virginia La Dart, 1946

A Message For Mother

If God had not created a more perfect woman,
then I could not call you "Mother".
And if my father had not picked such a perfect match,
then I would not even bother
to feel this sudden thrust to tell you why you are
celebrated in the lives of your children
and those who have followed them thus far.

It is amazing how you have kept such firm ground in this unstable world,
but from that ability I have gained direction unfurled.

I think of the early years so enticed by your beauty
now as well restored in your wisdom and admired by so many
of us who are proud to call you 'Mother' who's existence, by the way,
is forever appreciated like a cool summer day!

My Love

My Love,
If I blew up in a puff of smoke,
would you tend to cough and choke?

Love Is Trust

When you finally love - -
it's forever.

Crosses are always remembered - -
forever.

Faith constantly waits - -
forever.

Trust guilds the palace - -
forever.

This palace shall remain our home
forever.

Hurrying To Meet The Day

While the stars are shining - -
while the pines are pining,
passes twilight into day.
Then all men rise
making proper their ties
feigning - - "There's got to be an easier way."

They relate this to their creator
while contemplating the elevator - -
"LATE! Better take the stairs!"

Missing their first step,
then a fall
and bouncing back like a rubber ball - -
pretending no one sees or cares.

What God Has Given

Under the earth's crust
there's not a lot of dust
only matter extraordinarily weird.

Placing its usual region
particular to the season,
'nil more beautiful could be compared.

For this is God's land.
Works from his hands
do our bedazzled eyes behold.

What he has given through his love
from that source - - heaven above - -
Nature! Success with a weight of gold!

Logical Romance

We had to escape the chafe asserting our world
much of the time.
Wondered how far it would go - -
you on your planet,
and me on mine.

I've looked back on it with wit
or the lack of it
to find some kind of purpose,
but in that school of rationale
all reflection seems so worthless.

How do you treat a foolish heart?
How do you stop it from loving you so?
Probably just wiser to suffer the affliction
of pain in letting go.

You were the one that mattered,
and I refused to see you coming.
Now this defensive wall I've built
is all about me tumbling.

Sketching Nirvana

From me to you a gush of affection - -
Intimacy boils over stocking a well of good.
I love you as an observer loves detection,
and as romance loves a sultry mood.

How can I make you mine?
by hopes, dreams, wishes - - sweet wine?
Is there divinity in this madness?
That I await your summons, then crawl?

Fragments of this romance are piecing together,
but unfinished portions scream "glue".
If ever you decide to help make this dream greater,
then I swear that life will be progressively new!

Dawn 'Rainbow Girl' 1967

Dawn

God picked a star from his heavens
and placed it in this land.
He gave it life naming her Dawn,
and that became her brand.
For years we shared our lives
romping and giggling as young girls will do.
And I found this to be a perfect friend,
wouldn't you?

But soon we shoved our toys aside
and spats with little boys.
And a much different view of life appeared
which seemed to bring more joys.
We wiggled in and out of the weirdest mischief
that life could ever spare
while escaping parental punishment
by the ends of our tousled hair!
She had the most beautiful hazel eyes
and hair that shined so.
How it would glisten
in either sun, wind, rain, or snow.

I loved this friend, this friend of mine
with such fine qualities.
She performed loving deeds all the time
aiming just to please.
But early in my good friend's life
an illness came to pass.
So now she lives in the heavens above
in meadows of green, green grass.
This tragedy means naught to me
for I have sweet, sweet memories
which now give me pride to say
that Dawn was and still is a part of all of we.

Nowhere Over The Danger

Kilowatts weather the power of my love as I incredulously need you.
It's my belief in your person that makes hate seem untrue.

Coping with such thoughts mindfully propelling 'round and 'round - -
I note revenge plays no favor if there's a new love you've found.

Because a special happiness is all that I crave for your sweet being,
and composed behavior shall come easily if there's someone else you're seeing.

Time now to set this stage of our relationship in an unfading picture - -
of us out on a limb, nowhere over the danger.

The Blessed Ones

The Blessed Ones - -
How does one know?

By the clothing they wear?
Be it nunnery, vestments, or suit?
Casual, rags - - - what of 'Nothing'?

Would this be evil?
Do not the clothes wear the devil?

If the devil is dressed and only does misdeeds,
then is 'Naked' one of these?

Communication Breakdown

To what is it that I am listening?
Why is it that I do?
What is the temper of the news they are bringing?
Good, Bad, False, or True?

Sometimes we listen too much.
At times we catch the tail end.
Some use this end as a crutch,
and the beginning they start to mend.

From finish to start is easy to create,
but I would not advise it …
Maybe stories of fiction dealing with fate –
Reality is not to be fooled with.

Life is a treasure, not a toy.
Treat it with highest respect.
Living can bring so many joys,
which may also fall into shattered wrecks.

Please remember from this I wrote …
coming well from experience - -
There was someone to whom after I spoke
which resulted in undue weariness.

A Lonely World Without You

Your entity breathes into my memory, and loneliness sprouts from solitude of the truth -
that you are gone and yet still exist engulfed in your ideas - - cognizant of no one .

Die?

I shall not!

But, yea, as I park my harp on the right of my side, I play forlorn melodies while my head droops with a swan-like approach!

Shall I permit my tears to drown in the grassy lea?

Bid me to forebear my anguished sobs and direct my tarnished ego towards a more luminous episode in life!

Do not crowd me with this malicious departing which proves not only unreal to me but dead as a doornail besides!

You are bringing a doornail to life!

Only demons mar the code of living!

Angels do partake in foolish errors though - -

You are an angel.

I forgive you.

Milton Keynes UK
Ingram Content Group UK Ltd.
UKHW050412300124
436937UK00002B/50